SCHOLASTIC

READ & RESPOND

Helping children discover the pleasure and power of reading

Ellie and the CAT

MALORIE BLACKMAN

Illustrated by Matt Robertson

FOR AGES 7–9

Published in the UK by Scholastic Education, 2022

Scholastic Distribution Centre, Bosworth Avenue, Tournament Fields, Warwick, CV34 6UQ

Scholastic Ireland, 89E Lagan Road, Dublin Industrial Estate, Glasnevin, Dublin, D11 HP5F

SCHOLASTIC and associated logos are trademarks and/or registered trademarks of Scholastic Inc.

© 2022 Scholastic

www.scholastic.co.uk

1 2 3 4 5 6 7 8 9   2 3 4 5 6 7 8 9 0 1

Printed and bound by Ashford Colour Press
This book is made of materials from well-managed,
FSC®-certified forests and other controlled sources.

A CIP catalogue record for this book is available from the British Library.
ISBN 978-0702-31949-5

Due to the nature of the web, we cannot guarantee the content or links of any site mentioned. We strongly recommend that teachers check websites before using them in the classroom.

Author Sarah Snashall
Editorial team Rachel Morgan, Vicki Yates, Suzanne Adams and Julia Roberts
Series designer Andrea Lewis
Typesetter QBS Learning
Illustrator Yulia Gorkina

Photographs: page 8: Malorie Blackman, Barrington Stoke; page 18: Spanish castell, Natursports/Shutterstock; Dahi handi, Thesamphotography/Shutterstock; page 35: Kitten playing, Josep Suria/Shutterstock; Sphynx cat, Gladkova Svetlana/Shutterstock; Cats grooming, Karamysh/Shutterstock, Cat hunting, Maleo/Shutterstock

Acknowledgements
The publishers gratefully acknowledge permission to reproduce the following material:
Barrington Stoke Ltd for the use of the text extracts and cover from *Ellie and the Cat* Copyright © 1994 Oneta Malorie Blackman.
Every effort has been made to trace copyright holders for the works reproduced in this book, and the publishers apologise for any inadvertent omissions.

For supporting online resources go to:
www.scholastic.co.uk/read-and-respond/books/ellie-and-the-cat/online-resources
Access key: Work

CONTENTS ▼

How to use Read & Respond in your classroom...

Read & Respond provides teaching ideas related to a specific well-loved children's book. Each Read & Respond book is divided into the following sections:

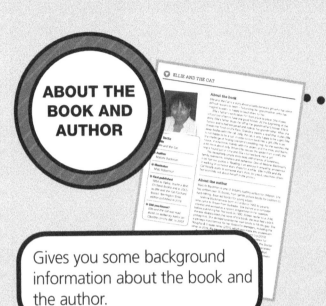

ABOUT THE BOOK AND AUTHOR

Gives you some background information about the book and the author.

GUIDED READING

Breaks the book down into sections and gives notes for using it, ideal for use with the whole class. A bookmark has been provided on page 12 containing **comprehension** questions. The children can be directed to refer to these as they read. Find comprehensive guided reading sessions on the supporting online resources.

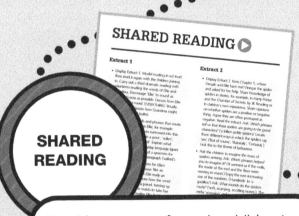

SHARED READING

Provides extracts from the children's book with associated notes for focused work. There is also one non-fiction extract that relates to the children's book.

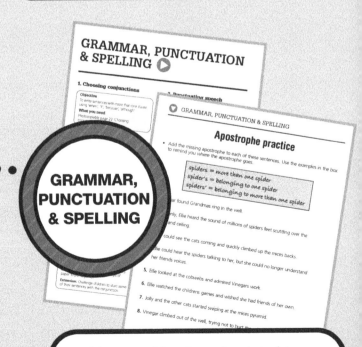

GRAMMAR, PUNCTUATION & SPELLING

Provides word-level work related to the children's book so you can teach grammar, punctuation, spelling and **vocabulary** in context.

PLOT, CHARACTER & SETTING

Contains activity ideas focused on the plot, characters and the setting of the story.

TALK ABOUT IT

Oracy, fluency, and speaking and listening activities. These activities may be based directly on the children's book or be broadly based on the themes and concepts of the story.

GET WRITING

Provides writing activities related to the children's book. These activities may be based directly on the children's book or be broadly based on the themes and concepts of the story.

ASSESSMENT

Contains short activities that will help you assess whether the children have understood concepts and curriculum objectives. They are designed to be informal activities to feed into your planning.

SUPPORTING ONLINE RESOURCE

Online you can find a host of supporting documents including planning information, comprehensive guided reading sessions and guidance on teaching reading.

www.scholastic.co.uk/read-and-respond/books/ellie-and-the-cat/online-resources
Access key: Work

Help children develop a love of **reading for pleasure.**

Activities

The activities follow the same format:

- **Objective:** the objective for the lesson. It will be based upon a curriculum objective, but will often be more specific to the focus being covered.

- **What you need:** a list of resources you need to teach the lesson, including photocopiable pages.

- **What to do:** the activity notes.

- **Differentiation:** this is provided where specific and useful differentiation advice can be given to support and/or extend the learning in the activity. Differentiation by providing additional adult support has not been included as this will be at a teacher's discretion based upon specific children's needs and ability, as well as the availability of support.

The activities are numbered for reference within each section and should move through the text sequentially – so you can use the lesson while you are reading the book. Once you have read the book, most of the activities can be used in any order you wish.

CURRICULUM LINKS

Section	Activity	Curriculum objectives
Guided reading		Comprehension: To develop positive attitudes to reading and understanding of what they read by listening to and discussing a wide range of fiction.
Shared reading	1	Comprehension: To draw inferences such as inferring characters' feelings, thoughts and motives from their actions, and to justify inferences with evidence.
	2	Comprehension: To discuss words and phrases that capture the reader's imagination; to identify themes and conventions.
	3	Comprehension: To identify themes and conventions; to identify main ideas drawn from more than one paragraph and summarise these; to identify how language, structure and presentation contribute to meaning.
	4	Comprehension: To retrieve and record information from non-fiction.
Grammar, punctuation & spelling	1	Vocabulary, grammar and punctuation: To extend the range of sentences with more than one clause by using a wider range of conjunctions including 'when', 'if', 'because', 'although'.
	2	Vocabulary, grammar and punctuation: To use and punctuate direct speech.
	3	Vocabulary, grammar and punctuation: To use conjunctions, adverbs and prepositions to express time and cause.
	4	Vocabulary, grammar and punctuation: To use fronted adverbials; to use commas after fronted adverbials.
	5	Comprehension: To use dictionaries to check the meaning of words they have read; to discuss their understanding and explain the meaning of words in context.
	6	Spelling: To place the possessive apostrophe accurately in words with regular plurals (for example, girls', boys') and in words with irregular plurals (for example, children's).
Plot, character & setting	1	Comprehension: To identify conventions in a wide range of books.
	2	Comprehension: To identify conventions in a wide range of books.
	3	Comprehension: To ask questions to improve their understanding of a text.
	4	Comprehension: To draw inferences such as inferring characters' feelings, thoughts and motives from their actions, and to justify inferences with evidence.
	5	Comprehension: To identify main ideas drawn from more than one paragraph and summarise these.
	6	Comprehension: To discuss words and phrases that capture the reader's interest and imagination.
	7	Comprehension: To discuss words and phrases that capture the reader's interest and imagination.
	8	Comprehension: To identify themes and conventions in a wide range of books.

Section	Activity	Curriculum objectives
Talk about it	1	Spoken language: To participate in discussions and presentations.
	2	Spoken language: To speak audibly and fluently with an increasing command of Standard English.
	3	Spoken language: To articulate and justify answers, arguments and opinions.
	4	Spoken language: To give well-structured narratives.
	5	Spoken language: To participate in collaborative conversations.
	6	Spoken language: To participate in role play; to ask relevant questions to extend their understanding and knowledge.
Get writing	1	Composition: To organise paragraphs around a theme; in non-narrative material, to use simple organisational devices.
	2	Composition: To compose and rehearse sentences orally…building an increasing range of sentence structures.
	3	Composition: To discuss writing similar to that which they are planning to write in order to understand and learn from its structure, vocabulary and grammar; to discuss and record ideas.
	4	Composition: To compose and rehearse sentences orally, progressively building a varied and rich vocabulary.
	5	Composition: In narratives, to create settings, characters and plot.
	6	Composition: To organise paragraphs around a theme; in non-narrative material, to use simple organisational devices.
Assessment	1	Composition: To build a varied and rich vocabulary.
	2	Vocabulary, grammar and punctuation: To use fronted adverbials.
	3	Vocabulary, grammar and punctuation: To extend the range of sentences with more than one clause by using a wider range of conjunctions including 'when', 'if', 'because', 'although'. Comprehension: To understand what they read in books they can read independently.
	4	Comprehension: To prepare poems and play scripts to read aloud and to perform, showing understanding through intonation, tone, volume and action.
	5	Comprehension: To identify themes and conventions.
	6	Comprehension: To predict what might happen from details stated and implied. Vocabulary, grammar and punctuation: To use and punctuate direct speech.

Key facts

⦿ **Title:**
Ellie and the Cat

⦿ **Author:**
Malorie Blackman

⦿ **Illustrator:**
Matt Robertson

⦿ **First published:**
1994 as Elaine, You're a Brat (Orchard Books) and in 2005 as Ellie and the Cat (Orchard Books). Barrington Stoke edition published in 2019.

⦿ **Did you know?**
Ellie and the Cat was read aloud on Jackanory Junior on CBeebies on the BBC in 2007.

About the book

Ellie and the Cat is a story about a badly-behaved girl who has some difficult lessons to learn – fortunately her grandmother, who has magical powers, is happy to teach them to her.

Ellie's father's work takes him from place to place. She moves school too often to have any good friends. At the beginning of the story, Ellie's father drops her off at her grandmother's house. Ellie is furious and is bad tempered and rude to her grandmother. After she throws her food on the floor, Grandma creates a spell that makes Ellie swap bodies with the cat. Jolly, the cat, is very happy to be a girl; Ellie is not happy to be a cat. In order to turn back into a girl, Ellie is set the challenge of finding Grandma's wedding ring. As she searches the house, she becomes friends with the spiders and the mice, and learns a bit more about Jolly. When Ellie rescues the spider from a well, the ring is found just in time and Ellie is turned back into a girl.

This deceptively simple story deals with themes of loneliness, family, teamwork, kindness and behaviour. One of Malorie Blackman's most famous quotes is 'Reading is an exercise in empathy; an exercise in walking in someone else's shoes for a while'. Ellie in Ellie and the Cat literally walks in someone else's shoes (or paws), sees how others feel and finds out about herself in the process.

About the author

Malorie Blackman is one of Britain's leading writers for children. She has written over 70 books, from gentle picture books for toddlers to hard-hitting, issue-led books for young adults.

Malorie Blackman was born in London in 1962 to parents who came to Britain from Barbados. She trained as a computer scientist and worked as a system programmer in her twenties before publishing her first book in 1990. A keen reader as a child, she was disappointed that none of the books she read had a black protagonist. She decided to write her own books to fill this gap. She is perhaps most famous for her fiction for teenagers, including the Noughts & Crosses series (2001), which was made into a television series in 2019, Pig Heart Boy (1997) and Boys Don't Cry (2010).

As well as writing novels, Malorie Blackman has written for television, including an episode of Doctor Who (in which the Doctor meets civil rights activist Rosa Parks) and Byker Grove. She received an OBE in 2008, a BAFTA in 2000 (for her play of Pig Heart Boy) and was Children's Laureate from 2013 to 2015. She has even been referenced in the lyrics of the singer Stormzy.

GUIDED READING ▶

Cover

Display the cover of the book and make predictions together. Discuss who the characters might be (a girl, a mouse, a cat and a spider, perhaps) and which of them might be Ellie. If possible, avoid reading the back-cover blurb to allow the magic to creep on up the children.

Chapter 1

Read the first few pages to '"He won't take me with him."' and locate verbs that describe Ellie's actions, for example: 'glared', 'kicking', 'yelling', 'shouted'. Ask a volunteer to read Ellie's direct speech. Ask: *What sort of character is Ellie?* (rude, mean, sulky) Discuss whether it is usual for the main character of a story to be so unpleasant. Read the rest of Chapter 1. Ask: *Has any new information changed your opinion of Ellie?* Share details such as, 'Ellie's eyes were stinging from unshed tears', 'alone and miserable', 'didn't have any close friends', 'felt like an unwanted parcel', 'yet another new school'. Share the children's thoughts about how it might feel to be Ellie. Discuss question 1 on the bookmark. Agree that she behaves badly because she is unhappy. Ask: *Is this any excuse for her behaviour?* Ask the children to reflect on their own behaviour when they are cross.

Move the focus onto Grandma. Locate information about how she looks, re-reading the description of her on the second page. Point out the noun phrases created by the author for hair, dress, glasses and eyes. Ask: *How does Grandma react to Ellie's behaviour?* (She is calm, she keeps smiling, but she frowns when Ellie can't see her.) *What might we infer about Grandma's character?* (She does not approve of Ellie's behaviour; she is probably not going to put up with it.) Ask: *What do we know that Ellie doesn't?* (That Grandma is watching her and is not impressed.) Discuss question 2 on the bookmark, suggesting answers such as 'Dad told her', 'It's a good guess'. Enjoy the rhythm of the list description at the end of this chapter: 'Ellie was sullen in the basement, sulked in the living room, scowled in the bedrooms and sighed in the attic.'

Chapter 2

Read up to 'flung everything on her plate under the table'. Establish that although Ellie has been given her favourite meal, she is still complaining. Discuss whether any version of sausage, beans and chips would have been good enough for her. Ask: *How does Ellie's behaviour get worse and worse?* First, she moans, then she plays with her food, then she is really rude, then she throws her food on the floor. Discuss what should happen to Ellie.

Read the rest of the chapter, then revisit question 2 on the bookmark. Share any new answers to this question. (For example, Grandma seems to be magic.) Speculate together how Grandma might teach Ellie a lesson. Look again at the cover for some clues.

Go back through the chapter and create a list of all the different words for something unpleasant in this chapter. (For example, 'Yuk', 'smelly', 'stinky', 'rotten', 'dreadful', 'nasty', 'greedy', 'rudest', 'disagreeable', 'brat'.)

Chapter 3

Together, read up to '"Don't talk wet!" Ellie laughed' and discuss the picture (if your edition has one). Agree that Grandma no longer seems to be the calm Grandma of Chapter 2. Speculate on why Ellie doesn't seem very scared at the beginning of this chapter. (Perhaps she doesn't believe that Grandma is really going to punish her; perhaps she has not realised that Grandma picked up the food using magic.) Ask: *What changes Ellie's mind?* (the thunder and lightning) Read the rest of the chapter. Find the order of events by which Ellie realises that she really has turned into a cat: first, she sees her body by the dinner table, then she sees her paws, then she sees her fur, then she realises she's walking on all fours, then she realises she's small, then she jumps up to the mirror, then she sees herself.

Discuss question 3 on the bookmark. Share different answers such as 'She lost her temper' or 'She wants Ellie to learn better manners'. Ask: *Why might being a cat teach Ellie some manners?* (She might start by learning not to be rude to Grandma, she might appreciate being a girl more, she might decide that she was lucky after all.) Establish that Grandma did not turn Ellie into a cat in order to find the ring – but that this was part of the spell. Ask: *How does Grandma feel about the spell?* (She seems quite relaxed, saying "Never mind". She also says she can't change Ellie back straight away and that she forgot there is a 'time limit'. She seems to feel Ellie might just need to get on with it.)

Chapter 4

Read the first two paragraphs of Chapter 4. Ask children who have or are familiar with cats to share their experiences of cat behaviour. Discuss whether 'wail' is a good word to describe the plaintive meow of a cat.

Read the next couple of pages. Make links to *The Gruffalo* by Julia Donaldson if the children know it, comparing the shadow trick used here and in *The Gruffalo*. Read question 10 on the bookmark. Ask: *Ellie has not really met Jolly but what can we/she infer about Jolly?* Locate all the names Dimple uses to describe Jolly: 'giant', 'sneaky', 'devious', 'sly', 'nasty', 'folly'. Ask: *Which of these words have similar meanings?* ('sneaky', 'devious', 'sly') Discuss what this tells us about Jolly. Ask: *What other horrible thing does Jolly do?* (plays with her food – the mice, before she eats them)

Ask: *What new experience does Ellie have in this chapter?* (She apologises for being rude.) *How else does her conversation with Dimple help her?* (She has to describe her actions.)

Chapter 5

Read the first page of Chapter 5 and talk about the attic setting. Ask: *Which nouns and adjectives create the impression of a spooky attic?* (nouns: 'cobwebs', 'moon'; adjectives: 'dark', 'dingy') Discuss the meaning of dingy. (dirty, dark and miserable) Read the next page and discuss the difference between Ellie's and the spider's opinions of the attic, locating vocabulary in the text, for example

'grubby and grimy' versus 'tip-top, minty-flinty'. Discuss question 11 on the bookmark. Clarify that 'minty-flinty' is a made-up term. Encourage the children to use context to guess what it means, adding in any other useful vocabulary knowledge. Point out that we sometimes use 'minty-fresh' to talk about clean teeth.

Find further words that are used to describe Jolly ('detestable', 'vile', 'awful', 'foul', 'spiteful', 'hateful'). Discuss the slightly different meaning of these words, linking meaning to the previous list. Ask: *Why is Ellie thoughtful when she hears Jolly described as 'rude and disagreeable and never thinks of anyone but herself'?* (She knows she could be described this way.) Discuss question 5 on the bookmark. (For example, hearing the animals talk about Jolly makes Ellie think of her own behaviour.) Ask: *Why does Ellie whisper when she tells the spiders that they are kind?* (She is feeling emotional, she is embarrassed because she is not used to people helping her.)

Find the description of the spiders coming to help Ellie. Ask: *Which phrases create the impression of millions of spiders?* ('soft, scurrying, scuttling noises', 'the walls…and the floor were moving in waves') Discuss question 12 on the bookmark and challenge the children to search through Chapter 5 to locate verbs that describe how Ellie ('padded') and Dimple ('scampered') move. Next, locate verbs that describe the arrival of Dimple's mouse friends: 'a rumbling and a tumbling and a pitter-pattering'.

Chapter 6

Read Chapter 6 up to 'We have a ring to find'. Ask: *What techniques does Malorie Blackman use to create the character of Jolly?* Agree she uses different verbs for 'said', such as' growled', 'purred', 'laughed', 'hissed'; she uses a repeated 'r', as in 'Yourrr frrrriends'; she makes Jolly behave in a cruel way.

Read the rest of the chapter. Then re-read the paragraph where the friends search the house. Point out how the author uses a list to quickly tell us what happens, with a repeated 'They'. Ask: *What other technique does she use here?* (rhyme) *Find the words that rhyme.* ('books'/'hooks', 'clock'/'rock', 'box'/'socks', 'everything'/'ring')

Chapter 7

Read the first half of the chapter. Ask a volunteer to answer question 6 on the bookmark. (By moving in a line, every part of the garden is searched carefully.) Ask: *What words would you use to describe how the animals work?* (teamwork, carefully, supportively, sensibly) Ask: *How might this experience be new for Ellie?* (She's not had friends before so perhaps she's not worked as part of a team.)

Ask: *How do we know that time is passing in this chapter?* (The sun moves from high to low in the sky.) Discuss question 7 on the bookmark. Help the children to remember that Ellie saw the moon through the attic window in Chapter 5 and sat in the morning sun in Chapter 6.

Read the rest of the chapter. Ask: *How do Ellie and Vinegar act in a selfless way in this chapter?* (Ellie tells the friends they can stop searching; Vinegar says the friends can leave her in the well while they keep searching.) Discuss questions 13 and 14 on the bookmark. Agree that Ellie has stopped only thinking of herself. Suggest that perhaps having friends who have supported her has made Ellie kinder. Debate whether saving Vinegar or searching for the ring is more important.

Point out that this story is set in a normal home. Look at question 15 on the bookmark. Agree that being small and being able to talk to animals changes the setting; having a dangerous villain (Jolly) also adds to the adventure.

Chapter 8

Read to '"We're going to get you out."'. Discuss question 4 on the bookmark. (Vinegar is her friend.) Ask: *What might be the result of this decision?* (Ellie might end up being a cat forever.) Ask: *Do you think she would have made this decision at the beginning of the story?* (Possibly not – she was too busy thinking of herself.) *What does this tell us?* (She is beginning to think of others; she is no longer so cross.) Ask the children to find another example of teamwork in this chapter.

Read the rest of the chapter. Ask: *Why don't any of the spiders complain when Vinegar treads on their heads?* (She's their friend and they are rescuing her.) Ask the children to find phrases that make Jolly and her friends seem sinister. ('sly smile', 'smirk'; repetition of 'They climbed… they covered…') Revisit question 5 on the bookmark. Point out that as well as showing Ellie a reflection of her own behaviour, having a 'baddie' adds excitement to the story.

Chapter 9

Read the first page. Find the alliteration ('big bully' and 'vile and vicious'). Ask: *Why is it worrying that the sun is so low, and Grandma is starting her dinner?* (Time is running out.) Read to the end, enjoying the final drama as Ellie and the mice race to outwit Jolly and the cats.

Afterwards, share final thoughts about the book. Ask: *How many happy endings are there?* (Grandma has her ring and a happy Ellie living with her; the mice are saved from Jolly; Ellie has learned how to be a friend; Ellie has a new, long-term home.) Ask: *Who doesn't have a happy ending?* (Jolly) Discuss how Jolly might be taught a lesson and speculate on the answer to question 16 on the bookmark.

Revisit question 1 on the bookmark. Ask: *How many of the things that made Ellie sad and cross have been solved?* (She will have friends, her father and a proper home.) Discuss question 17 on the bookmark. Agree that she might have more human and animal friends, that she might not want to (or think it is wise to) be rude to Grandma. Make a link between the answers to these questions.

Use question 8 to recap on the key events in the story. Next, discuss question 9. (In the attic she realises how people might see her and she understands what it is like to have a friend; in the garden she learns about teamwork; at the well she learns to put others before herself.) Move on to discuss question 18. (For example, kindness, friendship, teamwork, happiness, magic.)

Ellie and the Cat
By Malorie Blackman

Focus on...
Meaning

1. Why does Ellie behave so badly at the beginning of the story?

2. How does Grandma know what Ellie's new favourite foods are?

3. Why does Grandma turn Ellie into a cat?

4. Why does Ellie decide to save Vinegar?

Focus on...
Organisation

5. How important is Jolly to the story?

6. How is teamwork important to the plot?

7. How do we know that time is passing in the story?

8. What are the most important events in this story?

9. What lesson does Ellie learn in each setting?

Ellie and the Cat
By Malorie Blackman

Focus on...
Language and features

10. What is Jolly like?

11. What does 'minty-flinty' mean?

12. How does Malorie Blackman use verbs to create the impression of each animal?

Focus on...
Purposes, viewpoints and effects

13. How does Ellie's behaviour change?

14. Why does Ellie change?

15. How does Grandma's house become the setting for an adventure story?

16. What story would *Jolly and the Girl* be?

17. How will Ellie behave in the future?

18. What themes have you spotted in this story?

SHARED READING ▶

Extract 1

- Display Extract 1. Model reading it out loud, then read it again with the children joining in. Carry out a third dramatic reading with volunteers reading the words of Ellie and Grandma. Encourage 'Ellie' to sound as sulky and cross as possible. Discuss how Ellie might say the word 'EVERYTHING' (loudly; emphasised). Discuss how Grandma might sound in contrast (calm).

- Together, circle words and phrases that create the impression of cross Ellie, for example: 'kicked a stone', 'her eyes narrowed into thin slits', 'lips turned down in a pout', 'sullen', 'sulked', 'scowled', 'sighed'. Explain what 'sullen' means using everyday language (quiet and moody). Together, find a synonym for 'was sullen' in the same paragraph ('sulked').

- Ask: *Is there any justification for Ellie's behaviour?* Locate the phrase 'like an unwanted parcel'. Ask: *Is Ellie really an 'unwanted parcel'?* Explore how the word 'like' compares Ellie to a parcel, turning up at doors where no one wants to take her in. Discuss how this makes Ellie feel (even if Grandma and Dad do want her.) Locate other phrases that provide information about Ellie's feelings, for example, 'shunted back and forth', 'No one wanted her', 'tons and tons of nothing'. Ask: *Can you have 'tons of nothing'?* (Not really, but it is an effective phrase.) *What impression does this give?* (endless boring days)

- Ask a volunteer to read Ellie's wish. Discuss why this might be the thing Ellie wishes for. If you are reading it after you have finished the book, speculate on whether Grandma has made this wish come true – perhaps even on purpose.

Extract 2

- Display Extract 2, from Chapter 5, where Dimple and Ellie have met Vinegar the spider and asked for her help. Share knowledge of spiders in stories, for example, in *Harry Potter and the Chamber of Secrets*, by JK Rowling or in children's own experience. Share opinions on whether spiders are a positive or negative thing. Agree they are often portrayed as negative. Read the extract. Ask: *Which phrases tell us that these spiders are going to be good characters?* ('a trillion polite spiders)' Locate three different ways in which the spiders say 'yes' ('But of course', 'Naturally', 'Certainly'). Link this to the theme of behaviour.

- Ask the children to imagine the mass of spiders arriving. Ask: *Which phrases helped you to imagine it?* ('It seemed as if the walls, the inside of the roof and the floor were moving in waves') Enjoy the ever-increasing size of the numbers. ('Hundreds' to 'a gazillion') Ask: *What sounds do the spiders make?* ('soft, scurrying, scuttling noises'). The verbs 'scurrying' and 'scuttling' are used as adjectives here, but we can still picture them move. Ask: *What poetic techniques does Malorie Blackman use when describing the mice?* (rhyme, alliteration, exaggeration)

- Remind the children of Ellie's belief at the beginning of the story that there would be 'no one to play with, nothing to see, nothing to do' at Grandma's house. Discuss how Ellie might feel now (excited, supported, interested).

- Use the extract to recap on punctuating direct speech, for example: speech marks/inverted commas, a comma before the closing speech mark, a new line for a new speaker. Find two alternative words for 'said' ('replied', 'added').

Extract 3

- Display Extract 3, from the beginning of Chapter 9. Introduce the idea of the 'impossible task' story, sharing any that the children know such as 'Rumpelstiltskin'. Point out that in these stories the main character has to achieve an impossible goal by a certain time or something bad will happen. The main character often has help and might need to pass a test. Together, work out what these elements are for *Ellie and the Cat*. (She has to find a long-lost ring by the time her grandma finishes dinner, or she will remain as a cat; she is helped by the animals and proves that she is a kinder person than before – which she does by deciding to help Vinegar instead of looking for the ring.) Agree that at the end of task stories there is often a final challenge that makes it look as if all is lost.

- Read the extract aloud to the children, using expression to emphasise the drama. Then re-read the extract together, encouraging the children to copy your expression and pace.

- Agree that this is the climax of the story. Find the elements that add drama in the form of emotion, time running out or danger. For example, emotion: the characters are anxious ('Another ladder!', 'Come on! Faster', 'We don't have a moment to lose', 'Ellie chewed her lip', 'Quick'); time running out (the sun is going down, Grandma has started eating dinner); and danger (Jolly watching and then attacking).

- Ask the children to predict whether Ellie will succeed. Encourage them to explain their thinking. (The style of story suggests it will have a happy ending.)

Extract 4

- Display Extract 4. Challenge the children to find the link between the text and *Ellie and the Cat*. (The mice make a mouse pyramid; teamwork is a theme in *Ellie and the Cat*.) Read the text to the children and ask: *Why is teamwork so important when building a human tower?* (Everyone must keep balanced; everyone must take their share of the weight.) Ask: *Why must there be so many people on the bottom layer?* (to spread the weight) Search for and share videos online of these towers being formed, the pots being smashed and the towers falling.

- Ask volunteers to highlight the features of a non-fiction text. (headings, sub-headings, introduction, glossary, present-tense verbs, photographs, caption)

- Ask the children to find a sentence that links the introduction to the subheadings. Ask: *Can you explain how a tower is like a community? Why might the people from Catalonia, Spain and Hindus from India be the best human-tower builders in the world?* (It is part of their culture; they have competitions.)

- Find the key words and discuss the meaning of each. Ask: *Why is it important for the top child to be nimble?* (This will be apparent if you watch any videos of the final child climbing to the top.) Ask: *What else can you describe as 'nimble'?* (For example, a ballet dancer, a mountain goat, the fingers of a knitter, a cyclist weaving through traffic.)

- Apart from the arrival of a very large cat, what would make these towers dangerous? (For example, wind, one person in the middle losing their balance, a bird flying into the tower.)

Extract 1

Ellie felt like an unwanted parcel, being shunted back and forth between teachers and boring aunts and even some of Dad's friends. None of them really wanted her.

"It's not fair," Ellie said as she kicked a stone along the front path of Grandma's house. Now her dad had dumped her on her grandma, who didn't want her. No one wanted her. There'd be no one to play with, nothing to see, nothing to do. Ellie would have to put up with tons and tons of nothing for a whole month until she started yet another new school in September.

"I hate school, I hate this house, I hate EVERYTHING," Ellie said as her eyes narrowed into thin slits and her lips turned down in a pout. Then she whispered to herself, "I wish … I wish I could find someone who wants to be friends with me."

"Come along, Ellie," Grandma said as she stood at the front door. "Before we have dinner, I'll show you around my home, as it's just been redecorated and a lot of things have changed."

Grandma took Ellie all around the huge house. Ellie was sullen in the basement, sulked in the living room, scowled in the bedrooms and sighed in the attic.

"I don't want to do this any more," Ellie said. "I want my dinner, please."

"Very well then," Grandma said, and off they went to the dining room. But Ellie missed Grandma's frown as Grandma followed her down the stairs.

Extract 2

Almost right away, Ellie heard soft, scurrying, scuttling noises. Ellie looked around, surprised. It seemed as if the walls, the inside of the roof and the floor were moving in waves towards her. Then Ellie realised what it was.

Hundreds and thousands and millions of spiders.

"Um-hmm!" Vinegar cleared her throat for silence, then said, "Hello, friends. Ellie here needs our help to find her grandma's ring. She's been switched with Jolly the spiteful until she finds it. Will you all help?"

"But of course," one spider replied.

"Naturally," said another.

"Certainly," a third spider added.

The attic was filled with the noise of a trillion polite spiders all agreeing to help.

"Your turn, Dimple," Vinegar said.

"We'd better come out of the attic for this," Dimple said. "There isn't room in here for your friends and mine."

So Ellie, Dimple and Vinegar walked out of the attic, followed by a gazillion spiders. They reached the top of the steps that led down to the first floor and Dimple gave three low, long, loud whistles, making Ellie's ears jingle.

All of a sudden there came a rumbling and a tumbling and a pitter-pattering. The sound seemed to echo over the entire house. It seemed to Ellie that every mouse in the world was coming up the stairs.

Extract 3

Ellie looked up at the sky. The sun was very low. Ellie could see Grandma sitting by her open window, just starting her dinner.

"Another ladder!" Dimple said. "We don't need to use the door. We can make another ladder of mice going up the wall to your grandma. Come on, everyone. We don't have a moment to lose."

"You'll neverrrr do it in time," Jolly said, and crossed her arms.

The mice ignored Jolly and clambered to make a ladder up the wall towards Grandma's window. Ellie watched, feeling worried. A row of mice stood under Grandma's window, then more mice got on top of them, then more mice got on top of them. The pyramid of mice grew quickly.

"Come on! Faster!" Dimple shouted.

The pyramid was halfway up the wall. The sun was getting lower. Ellie chewed her lip. What would happen?

"Quick, Ellie, start climbing," Dimple called out.

Ellie bounded up the pyramid, climbing higher and higher.

She had to be careful not to hurt the mice she was stepping on.

Jolly walked out into the garden to see what was happening. "Frrrriends, quick. I need your help," Jolly called. "Ellie is almost at herrrr grrrrandma's window."

The mice climbed faster to build the pyramid higher. Ellie was a metre away from her grandma's open window.

"Get them! Get them!" Jolly hissed. She tore at the pyramid of mice with her hands. The pyramid began to sway, then to rock, as Jolly pulled mice away from it.

Extract 4

Human towers

To create a tall and safe human tower, the athletes must work together as a team. The highest human towers can have nine or ten layers of people and are made by teams in India and Spain.

Spanish castells

In Catalonia, Spain, athletes build human towers called *castells*. Every two years **colles castelleres** (teams that build towers) compete against each other at the Human Tower Competition in Tarragona, Spain. A huge group of strong men link arms to form a strong **base**. Rings of climbers form above them until a single young child climbs to the top. This child must be brave, light and **nimble**.

The towers represent the **community**: strong, older people hold up the children. The **motto** of the **castelleres** (tower builders) is 'Strength, balance, courage and common sense'.

A child about to smash the dahi handi.

Dahi Handi

At the Hindu festival of Dahi Handi, a *dahi handi* (a clay pot filled with **curd** and **ghee**) is hung across a street or attached to the end of a crane. Groups of human towers complete to reach the pot and smash it. When the pot is smashed, the climbers are covered with sweet curd and ghee.

base – the bottom of a building
castells – towers (Catalan)
colles castelleres – tower builders (Catalan)
community – people who live in the same area and support each other

curd – a type of yoghurt
ghee – a type of butter from India
motto – a saying linked to a particular group
nimble – can climb easily and quickly

GRAMMAR, PUNCTUATION & SPELLING ▶

1. Choosing conjunctions

Objective
To write sentences with more than one clause using 'when', 'if', 'because', 'although'.

What you need
Photocopiable page 22 'Choosing conjunctions'.

What to do

- Write the following sentences on the board (leaving spaces as shown by the forward slashes): 'The spiders will help Ellie / because / they don't like Jolly.'; 'The spiders will help Ellie / although / Ellie is a cat.'; 'The spiders will help Ellie / when / she says sorry for being rude.'; 'The spiders will help Ellie / if / she asks them.'. Then work with the children to locate the clauses and conjunctions.

- Together, play around with the order of the clauses and conjunctions, for example: 'Because they don't like Jolly, the spiders help Ellie.'

- Investigate what happens to the meaning of the sentences when the conjunction is changed, for example: 'The spiders help Ellie although they don't like Jolly'.

- Ask the children, in pairs, to cut out the conjunctions and clauses on photocopiable page 22 'Choosing conjunctions' and create as many different sentences as they can, writing them in their books. Remind them to change the punctuation and capital letters where necessary.

- Provide the following sentence: 'The mice will search the garden.' Ask the children, working in pairs, to use the conjunctions 'because', 'although', 'when' and then 'if' to add a second clause to the sentence.

Differentiation
Support: Provide children with the clauses and sentences in the starter on strips of paper to put together.

Extension: Challenge children to start some of their sentences with the conjunction.

2. Punctuating speech

Objective
To use and punctuate direct speech.

What you need
Copies of *Ellie and the Cat*, photocopiable page 23 'Punctuating speech'.

What to do

- Re-read the first three pages of Chapter 6 together (up to '"Ow!!!" Jolly yelled.') two or three times, asking different children to take on the roles of Ellie, Dimple, Vinegar, Jolly and Lad-luggens. Encourage them to bravely engage with the character and show emotion as they speak. Use the words for 'said' to infer how the characters feel ('snorted', 'laughed', 'purred', 'shouted', 'squeaked'). Discuss the meaning of 'snorted' here (said while laughing because someone has said something ridiculous).

- Ask volunteers to use the text to explain the correct punctuation for direct speech.

- With the children's help, make up a couple of extra lines with two different speakers to add to this conversation – perhaps Dimple tells Lad-luggens to run, or Lad-luggens shouts an insult to Jolly. For example: '"Quick, Lad! Run!"' shouted Dimple. '"Phew! That was close," gasped Lad-luggens. "I thought I was Jolly's dinner!"'

- Scribe for the children, asking them to tell you what punctuation to use as you write.

- Provide individual children with photocopiable page 23 'Punctuating speech' and ask them to rewrite the passage using correct punctuation (including a new line for a new speaker).

Differentiation
Support: Children should work in pairs to highlight the words spoken before they tackle the punctuation individually.

Extension: Encourage children to continue the scene on the sheet with a few more lines of dialogue.

3. Time passes

Objective

To use conjunctions, adverbs and prepositions to express time.

What you need

Copies of *Ellie and the Cat*.

What to do

- Provide the children with individual copies of *Ellie and the Cat* for reference. Working in pairs, ask the children to tell their partner a synopsis of the story. Encourage them to use a range of time words including conjunctions ('when'), adverbs ('next', 'later', 'eventually', 'after'), adverbials ('when the sun went down', 'a few minutes later') and prepositions ('before', 'after', 'to', 'by'), writing a range on the board if helpful.

- Taking ideas from different volunteers, create a shared writing synopsis of the story. Read a first draft together, discussing places where further words for time will help the synopsis to flow. Create a revised version, for example: 'Ellie **always** moves from place to place. **When** Ellie is left at her grandma's she is very upset. **As soon as she arrives**, she behaves badly and **before long** her grandma is cross. **When** Ellie drops her food on the floor, Grandma swaps Ellie's body with Jolly the cat. Ellie must find Grandma's ring **before** the sun goes down in order to become a girl again. **First**, Ellie meets a mouse call Dimple. **Then**, Ellie and Dimple meet a spider called Vinegar. The friends search the whole house **while** Jolly watches them **constantly**. **Finally**, they go out into the garden and **eventually** Vinegar finds the ring in a well. **Just as the sun sets**, Ellie leaps through the window and delivers the ring to Grandma.'

- Delete the shared writing and challenge the children to write their own short synopsis using a range of time words.

Differentiation

Support: Support children with a range of words and phrases to use.

Extension: Ask children to share their synopsis with the class.

4. Before the sun goes down

Objectives

To use fronted adverbials; to use commas after fronted adverbials.

What you need

Copies of *Ellie and the Cat*.

What to do

- Challenge the children, in pairs, to locate a sentence that starts with a fronted adverbial in Chapter 1 of *Ellie and the Cat*. ('As a result, Ellie had lived in more houses and been to more schools than she could remember.') Use it to recap on what a fronted adverbial is. (A phrase, that works like an adverb, that is placed at the beginning of a sentence.) Point out the comma. Clarify that the sentence makes sense without the adverbial.

- Challenge the pairs to come up with a replacement adverbial for the sentence, for example, 'Over the years', 'Sadly for her', 'Before long'. Write the new sentence with one of the suggested adverbials, correctly punctuated.

- Set the children to gather fronted adverbials from the book, for example: Chapter 1: 'Before we have dinner'; Chapter 4: 'Mind you'; Chapter 5: 'Almost right away', 'All of a sudden'; Chapter 6: 'At the foot of the stairs'; Chapter 7: 'Slowly, oh so slowly'; Chapter 8: 'As Ellie watched', 'At last' 'Then slowly and surely'; Chapter 9: 'As soon as your feet touch the carpet', 'Immediately', 'Now then', 'So when he gets back'.

- Ask the children, working individually, to choose five of the adverbials from their list and write a new sentence of their own for each one.

Differentiation

Support: Write the sentences from the book on strips of paper, then cut off the fronted adverbials. Provide the children with the fronted adverbials to find in the book. Then, challenge them to put the sentences back together.

Extension: Challenge children to tell you want sort of information each fronted adverbial provides – time, cause or manner.

5. Jolly the sly

Objectives
To use dictionaries to check the meaning of words; to discuss their understanding and explain the meaning of words in context.

What you need
Copies of *Ellie and the Cat*, dictionaries.

What to do

- Challenge pairs to remember two names that Dimple calls Jolly, writing these on their whiteboards and holding them up (for example 'Jolly the sly', 'Jolly the sneaky').

- Ask the pairs to scan *Ellie and the Cat* for all the adjectives used to complete the name 'Jolly the…' in the story. (For example, 'giant', 'sneaky', 'devious', 'sly', 'nasty', 'folly', 'horrid', 'detestable', 'vile', 'awful', 'foul', 'spiteful', 'hateful', 'creep', 'dreadful', 'revolting'.)

- Define any unfamiliar words such as 'devious', 'folly' and 'detestable' using everyday language and provide examples in simple sentences from different contexts.

- Then challenge pairs to discuss all the words. Ask: *Which words mean the same?* Encourage them to use a dictionary to check meanings.

- Ask pairs to sort the words into sets with similar meaning. (For example, 'sneaky', 'devious', 'sly', 'creep'; 'nasty', 'horrid', 'detestable', 'vile', 'awful', 'spiteful', 'hateful', 'dreadful'; 'foul', 'revolting'; 'giant'; 'folly'.)

- Share the lists and discuss any differences among them. Ask: *Is 'spiteful' sly enough to make it into the 'sly' list? Have you put 'foul' and 'revolting' in their own list or together in the 'nasty' list?* Ask: *Which words are only used for people (and animals)? Which words can be used for other nouns such as food or smells?*

- Ask the children to choose three of the words and create their own sentences for each one.

Differentiation
Support: Provide the words as cards to sort.

Extension: Challenge children to find and list other adjectives used to describe Jolly, for example: 'rude', 'disagreeable', 'evil', 'rotten', 'lying toad', 'vile', 'vicious'. Ask the children to use them in their own sentences.

6. Apostrophe practice

Objective
To place the possessive apostrophe accurately in words with regular and irregular plurals.

What you need
Photocopiable page 24 'Apostrophe practice'.

What to do

- Write the following sentences on the board and use them to recap on the rules of using an apostrophe: 'Ellie threw her <u>sausages</u> on the floor.' (plural noun; no possession); 'Ellie saw a giant <u>mouse's</u> shadow.' (single noun with possession – the shadow belongs to the mouse); 'Ellie admired the <u>cobwebs'</u> beauty.' (plural noun with possession – the cobwebs have beauty); 'The <u>mice's</u> feet pounded the stairs.' (irregular plural noun with possession – the feet belong to the mice).

- Work together to correctly punctuate the following sentences, locating singular/plural, possession/plural and irregular/regular nouns: 'The childrens voices could be heard in the playground.'; 'The mices nests were made from feathers.'; 'The spiders foot was stuck in the slime.'; 'Ellie could see Jolly and her friends coming.'; 'Ellie was scared by the cats arrival. There were so many of them!'

- Discuss the punctuation needed for the following sentence: 'Ellie needed the spiders help.' Agree that there is not enough information in the sentence for us to know how many spiders there are. Clarify with each of the following and punctuate accordingly:

  - 'Ellie looked at the millions of spiders. She needed the spiders help.' (spiders' help)
  - 'Ellie looked at Vinegar. She needed the spiders help.' (spider's help)

- Ask the children to complete photocopiable page 24 'Apostrophe practice', warning them to watch out for simple plurals.

Differentiation
Support: Provide children with the photocopiable page with the plurals highlighted in one colour and the words that need an apostrophe in another colour. Ask them to add the apostrophes independently.

Extension: Challenge children to write their own sentences that include plural apostrophes.

Choosing conjunctions

- Cut out the boxes and use them to create sentences.
- Try changing the conjunction in your sentence to change its meaning.
- Now try moving the conjunction and the box that follows it to the beginning of the sentence.
- Write down all the sentences you create.

Grandma puts a spell on Ellie	when	she is rude.
Ellie is cross	because	her father leaves her at Grandma's.
Ellie will stay as a cat	if	she doesn't find the ring.
Ellie rescues Vinegar	although	she needs to find the ring.
Vinegar finds the ring	when	she falls in the well.
The mice do not like Jolly	because	Jolly is mean.
Jolly will be in trouble	if	she is mean to the mice.
Ellie stops looking for the ring	although	the sun is going down.

Punctuating speech

- Rewrite this text below. Add speech marks. Remember to use a new line for a new speaker.

Just then, Jolly appeared around the corner. Who shall I eat first? she purred. Yum – this one looks tasty. You're not eating me, squeaked Dimple. You're not eating any of us. Let's see about that, she said, grabbing Dimple's tail. Help! cried Dimple. Vinegar – I need your help. We're coming, called Vinegar as the spiders entered the hall. They covered the floor and the ceiling. They ran up Jolly's legs. They ran up Jolly's arms. Arrgh, screamed Jolly, dropping Dimple. Get off!

_____

_____

_____

_____

_____

_____

_____

_____

_____

_____

_____

_____

_____

Apostrophe practice

- Add the missing apostrophe to each of these sentences. Use the examples in the box to remind you where the apostrophe goes.

> spiders = more than one spider
> spider's = belonging to one spider
> spiders' = belonging to more than one spider

1. Vinegar found Grandmas ring in the well.

2. Suddenly, Ellie heard the sound of millions of spiders feet scuttling over the walls and ceiling.

3. Ellie could see the cats coming and quickly climbed up the mices backs.

4. Ellie could hear the spiders talking to her, but she could no longer understand her friends voices.

5. Ellie looked at the cobwebs and admired Vinegars work.

6. Ellie watched the childrens games and wished she had friends of her own.

7. Jolly and the other cats started swiping at the mices pyramid.

8. Vinegar climbed out of the well, trying not to hurt the spiders heads with her feet.

PLOT, CHARACTER & SETTING ▶

1. A quest story

> **Objective**
> To identify the conventions of a quest story.
>
> **What you need**
> Copies of *Ellie and the Cat*, photocopiable page 29 'A quest story'.

What to do

- Discuss any quest stories that the children know, for example, *Finding Nemo*. Together, fill in an enlarged version of photocopiable page 29 'A quest story' for your chosen story. (For example, bad event: Nemo is captured; task: to find Nemo; a helper: Dory; an enemy: the sharks; a brave act: going into the open ocean; time constraint: Nemo is about to be given away as a gift; if the hero (Marlin) fails: Marlin will lose Nemo.

- Suggest that although *Ellie and the Cat* takes place in Grandma's house, it is also a quest story. Challenge pairs to discuss this.

- Provide the children with the photocopiable sheet to complete. Share answers, for example: a bad event: Grandma loses her temper; a quest: to find Grandma's ring; a helper: Dimple and Vinegar; an enemy: Jolly; a brave act: Ellie decides to help Vinegar; a time constraint: she must find the ring before the end of dinner the next day; if the hero fails: Ellie will remain a cat.

- Ask the children to use the information on their sheet to describe *Ellie and the Cat* to a partner.

> **Differentiation**
> **Support:** Provide children with the answers and ask them to stick them into the correct places in the table.
>
> **Extension:** Challenge children to present a polished version of their oral story, adding adjectives and adverbs for atmosphere and flow.

2. Adventure setting

> **Objective**
> To identify conventions of an adventure story setting.
>
> **What you need**
> Copies of *Ellie and the Cat*.

What to do

- Discuss together the type of settings that you might find in an adventure story (mountains, swamps, castles, caves and so on). Ask: *How does Grandma's house become an adventure story setting?* Agree that when Ellie becomes a cat, the house becomes much more challenging for her. Ask the children to imagine the house as an adventure setting. Ask: *What does Ellie find?* (the shadow of a giant, a spooky moonlit attic, a dangerous enemy, a stinky well, a tall wall)

- Draw on the board a cut-away version of Grandma's house with the garden and the well next to it. Ask the children to copy this and to add the characters in each room. They then label the different elements in their picture, adding noun phrases from the book, or from their own ideas. (For example, 'the shadow of an enormous beast', 'dark and dingy attic covered in cobwebs', 'the roof and the floor were moving in waves towards her', 'every mouse in the world was coming up the stairs', 'a well with slippery and slimy walls', 'a slimy stink coming from the well', 'Cats and more cats appeared from behind Jolly until they filled the doorway', 'leapt through the window'.)

> **Differentiation**
> **Support:** Discuss ideas as a class before children label the picture by themselves. Limit the number of labels they need to provide.
>
> **Extension:** Ask children to create longer descriptive phrases.

PLOT, CHARACTER & SETTING

3. Questions for Grandma

Objective
To ask questions to improve their understanding of the character of Grandma.

What you need
Copies of *Ellie and the Cat*, sticky notes.

Cross-curricular link
PSHE

What to do

- Explain that you are going to focus on Grandma. Together, re-read the key parts where she appears (Chapters 1, 2, 3, 6 and 9) and discuss any images of her in your edition.

- Ask groups of four to find the paragraphs beginning 'Ellie lifted her head…' (Chapter 1), '"Don't talk wet…"' (Chapter 3), '"My wedding ring…"' and 'Ellie couldn't believe it…' (both Chapter 9) and mark them with sticky notes. They then read the paragraphs aloud, taking a paragraph each.

- Ask the groups to suggest as many questions as they can about Grandma for each of these points in the story. For example: Chapter 1: How does she feel about Ellie coming to stay? Does she hear what Ellie says about her? Chapter 3: Is she really a witch? Has she really met a dragon? Challenge them to speculate on an answer for each question. Clarify that they can use evidence from later in the book (Grandma hugs Ellie) to answer questions at the beginning, such as 'Is she pleased to see Ellie?'

- Share the questions and any answers the children have discussed. Talk about which questions they were able to infer an answer to and which they could not. (Keep a note of children's ideas to use in 'A hot seat for Grandma', page 34.)

- Ask the children, working independently, to write a description of Grandma, including what she looks like, what she is like and how she feels, bringing together ideas across the book.

Differentiation
Support: Ask children to draw a picture of Grandma and write a caption.

Extension: Encourage children to write a detailed description that includes interesting vocabulary from the story.

4. What is she like?

Objective
To infer Ellie's feelings, thoughts and motives from her actions, and to justify inferences with evidence.

What you need
Copies of *Ellie and the Cat*, photocopiable page 30 'What is she like?'.

What to do

- Provide children with individual copies of *Ellie and the Cat*. Ask a volunteer to describe Ellie at the beginning of the story. Challenge them to talk in detail, remembering what Ellie does and why. Ask all the children to search through their copy of *Ellie and the Cat* for one example of Ellie's bad behaviour.

- Then ask another volunteer to talk about Ellie at the end of the story, describing her behaviour in detail, before asking all the children to search for evidence.

- Provide children with photocopiable page 30 'What is she like?'. Ask them to write their answers, finding as many pieces of evidence from the text as they can.

- Share answers. For example, at the beginning, Ellie is bad tempered; evidence: she crosses her arms, is rude to Grandma, sulks, scowls, throws her food on the floor. She is lonely and feels unloved; evidence: she feels like an 'unwanted parcel'; she wishes for a friend. At the end, Ellie is happy and kind; evidence: she rescues Vinegar, she hugs Grandma, she says sorry. She feels loved by Grandma and her friends who have all helped her even when it is dangerous; evidence: she can understand her friends, she is happy to stay with Grandma.

- Ask: *What has made Ellie change?* Agree that it is having friends who are willing to help her.

Differentiation
Support: Ask children to discuss their answers and find evidence in pairs, before writing their responses individually.

Extension: Ask children to discuss whether Ellie will stay happy or go back to her old ways, giving reasons.

5. Cause and effect

Objective
To identify main ideas drawn from more than one paragraph and summarise these.

What you need
Copies of *Ellie and the Cat*, photocopiable page 31 'Cause and effect'.

What to do

- Ask: *How does Ellie feel at the beginning of the story?* (cross, sad, lonely) *How does she feel at the end of the story?* (happy) *Why is Ellie happy at the end?* (She has friends, she is going to stop moving around, she has found the ring.) Ask: *How did Ellie feel when she was turned into a cat?* (cross, horrified) *Was being turned into a cat a good or a bad thing for Ellie?* (a good thing) *Why?* (She learned to behave better, she made friends, she made Grandma happy.) Agree that Ellie was happy at the end because she had turned into a cat.

- Recap on previous work done on combining sentences using 'because', by combining the sentences 'Ellie was happy at the end.' and 'Ellie had turned into a cat.'

- Write the sentence 'Vinegar fell in the well.' Together, extend this sentence using 'because'. For example, 'Vinegar fell in the well because she was jumping up and down to persuade the others to help Ellie.' or 'Because she fell in the well, Vinegar found the ring.' Introduce the terms 'cause' (the first event) and 'effect' (the second event).

- Provide pairs with photocopiable page 31 'Cause and effect'. Ask them to combine the sentences using 'because' to make up oral sentences, writing down their five favourites. They can use any sentence more than once. Remind the children that when combining the sentences, they will need to replace nouns with pronouns.

Differentiation
Support: Provide children with fewer sentences to combine.

Extension: Challenge children to write their own cause and effect sentences using different aspects of the plot.

6. The creepy, dusty attic

Objective
To discuss words and phrases that capture the reader's interest and imagination.

What you need
Copies of *Ellie and the Cat*, images of attics and cobwebs.

What to do

- Explain that you will be focusing on the attic and the language Malorie Blackman uses to bring it to life in our minds.

- Ask volunteers to read aloud Chapter 5 to '"So now Jolly is in my body and I'm in hers."' Point out that Ellie and Vinegar see the attic differently. Discuss any new vocabulary using everyday language. For example, 'dingy' (dark and miserable), 'skylight' (a window in a roof), 'jumble' (pile of old things), 'tip-top' (the best), 'minty-flinty' (made up but perhaps means clean and new), 'grubby' (dirty), 'grimy' (dirty), 'yucky' (horrible), 'icky' (revolting), 'tapestries' (cloth pictures), 'patience' (taking time), 'artistry' (with clever artistic skills).

- Ask the children to divide a piece of landscape paper headed 'The attic' in half and label one half 'Ellie's attic' and the other 'Vinegar's attic'. They then copy words and phrases from the text into the appropriate column and draw an accompanying picture of each attic (one abandoned and dirty; one clean and artistically decorated). For example: Ellie's attic: 'Dark and dingy and full of cobwebs. The only light came from the moon trying to shine in through the skylight above them.', 'jumble', 'grubby and grimy and full of yucky-icky cobwebs'; Vinegar's attic: 'tip-top, minty-flinty condition', 'silk tapestries', 'woven with care and skill, patience and artistry, love'. Display images of dusty attics and beautiful, complete cobwebs for support.

Differentiation
Support: Provide descriptive phrases on cards for the children to sort and stick into two columns.

Extension: Use the new vocabulary from the text to write an extended description of the attic from either Ellie's or Vinegar's point of view.

7. Animal behaviour

Objective
To discuss words and phrases that capture the reader's interest and imagination.

What you need
Copies of *Ellie and the Cat*.

Cross-curricular link
Science

What to do

- Recap on the different animals in *Ellie and the Cat* (spiders, mice, cats). Challenge the children to suggest words that might describe how these animals move. (For example, spiders: 'scuttle'; mice: 'scamper'; cats: 'pad'.)

- Ask pairs to create lists of verbs and phrases that capture how the different animals move. Tell them to organise the words into four lists: 'Spiders', 'Mice', 'Ellie the cat' and 'Jolly the girl'. For example:

  - Spiders: 'patter of lots of tiny feet', 'soft, scurrying, scuttling noises', 'moving in waves', 'fled', 'scampered', 'jumped up and down… waving all of her arms and legs', 'trampled'.

  - Mice: 'opened his eyes and stared', 'a rumbling and a tumbling and a pitter-pattering', 'squeaks and squeals', 'screamed', 'scampering', 'wriggling and jiggling', 'nipping', 'sniffing and scratching', 'clambered'.

  - Ellie the cat: 'stretched', 'sprang', 'wailed', 'stretched out her claws', 'lay down with her head on her front paws', 'leapt', 'stretching out'.

  - Jolly the girl (but still behaves like a cat): 'bent her head to lick', 'my prrrretty one', 'lifted the mouse over her mouth and dangled it there'.

  - Bring the class back together to share lists. Ask volunteers to say their favourite word or phrase and why they like it.

Differentiation
Support: Ask children to find and copy one phrase that they like for each list.

Extension: Ask children to locate other, non-spider/mice things that create the characters of Vinegar and Dimple. (For example, Vinegar is house-proud and has a 'squeaky voice'; Dimple is brave and says 'bloomin''.)

8. Theme of friendship

Objective
To explore the theme of friendship in *Ellie and the Cat*.

What you need
Copies of *Ellie and the Cat*.

Cross-curricular link
PSHE

What to do

- Challenge the children to remember what Ellie wishes for in Chapter 1 (a friend). Ask: *Does Ellie's wish come true? How?* (Yes; she makes friends with the spiders and the mice.)

- Ask the children, in small groups, to discuss friendship and what it means to them. Share ideas such as: friends help us, we have fun with our friends, friends make us feel we belong, friends can teach us things, friends look after each other. Write key words on the board.

- Ask the groups to discuss the theme of friendship in *Ellie and the Cat*. Tell the children, in their group, to write the word 'Friendship' in their books and to write notes on the theme. Suggest that they organise their ideas into areas based on the class discussion such as 'help', 'belong', 'teach', 'look after'. (Point out that Ellie doesn't have time to have fun with her friends.) Ask them to find all the places in the story where friendship is important and note these. For example, 'help': the spiders and the mice help Ellie to find the ring, the friends help each other to get the ring to Grandma; 'belong': Ellie's animal friends make her feel that Grandma's house is her home at the end of the story; 'teach': Vinegar and Dimple show Ellie how to be better; 'look after': Ellie gives up looking for the ring in order to help Vinegar, the spiders let Vinegar tread on them.

Differentiation
Support: Provide the children with a set of statements to sort.

Extension: Ask children to present to the class why bravery is an important theme in the story.

A quest story

- How is the story like an adventure story? Complete the table.

A bad event that starts the story	
A task	
A helper	
An enemy	
A brave act	
A time constraint	
What will happen if the hero fails?	

What is she like?

- In the boxes in the middle of the page, draw Ellie at the beginning and end of the story. Then write notes about her at each stage.

What is Ellie like?

Evidence:

What is Ellie like?

Evidence:

Ellie at the end

Ellie at the beginning

Why is Ellie like this?

Evidence:

Why is Ellie like this?

Evidence:

Cause and effect

- Cut out these sentences. Pair up the sentences as a cause and effect, then combine the two sentences using 'because'.
- Make up as many sentences as you can. Write down at least five.

Vinegar fell in the well.	Ellie was rude to Grandma.
Ellie was turned into a cat.	Vinegar was excited and jumped too high.
Vinegar did not like Jolly.	Ellie said sorry to Dimple.
The spiders and the mice could help Ellie.	Ellie needed help to find Grandma's ring.
Vinegar wanted to help Ellie.	The spiders and the mice worked as a team.
Dimple became Ellie's friend.	Jolly was mean to the animals.
Ellie made friends with the spiders and mice.	Vinegar found the ring.

TALK ABOUT IT ▶

1. All about cats

> **Objective**
> To participate in discussions and presentations.
> **What you need**
> Photocopiable page 35 'All about cats', books about cats, internet access.
> **Cross-curricular link**
> Science

What to do

- Ask the children to share anecdotes about cats they know or have. Pause for a moment for the children to gather their thoughts, then encourage them to talk in clear, full sentences using precise language.

- Ask mixed-ability groups to plan, research and give a two-minute presentation about cats. Provide each group with photocopiable page 35 'All about cats' to help them get started. Ask them, as a group, to choose one question to find out about and present on. They could use one of the ideas from the photocopiable page or an idea of their own. Provide books and supported internet access. Remind the children that they can also use their own knowledge.

- Ask them to create cards, boards or slides for their presentation and to use images from the photocopiable page or from the internet (or images of their own cats).

- Tell them to practise their presentation, helping each other know when to speak and checking that they are speaking clearly. Expect every child to have a clear role.

- Share the presentations in turn. Encourage the children to ask questions at the end of each presentation. (Keep children's notes for the Get writing on page 40.)

> **Differentiation**
> **Support:** Provide sentence starters for the presentation ('Kittens like to…', 'Often, cats…').
>
> **Extension:** Ask children to research more questions from the sheet.

2. Reading aloud

> **Objective**
> To read aloud fluently and dramatically.
> **What you need**
> Copies of *Ellie and the Cat*.

What to do

- Re-read Chapter 1 (or part of Chapter 1) out loud, modelling the different techniques we use to read aloud fluently and dramatically. Afterwards, work with the children to create a list of reading-aloud techniques on the board. (For example, reading at a controlled pace, putting on different voices for different characters, pausing dramatically occasionally, changing the volume appropriately, looking at the audience and so on.)

- Then read a small section again before asking pairs to take turns to re-read it to their partner, using the strategies you have modelled.

- Provide the children with individual copies of *Ellie and the Cat* and ask them to prepare a few pages to read aloud to the class or group. Suggest suitable passages such as the beginning of Chapter 3, the beginning of Chapter 5 or the middle of Chapter 6, including the list of the items found.

- Ask the children to read their chosen section with a partner, talking about where different techniques can be used. Remind them to check that they understand each word and what the passage is about before attempting a dramatic reading. Ask them to take turns reading to each other and giving advice for improvement.

- Share their performances.

> **Differentiation**
> **Extension:** Encourage children to perform a longer passage.

3. Whose fault?

Objective
To articulate and justify answers, arguments and opinions.

What you need
Copies of *Ellie and the Cat*, photocopiable page 36 'Whose fault?'

Cross-curricular link
PSHE

What to do

- Ask: Why is Ellie turned into a cat? (Because she was rude to Grandma.) Ask: *Why was Ellie rude to Grandma?* (Because she was sad about being left by her father.) Ask: *Why did Ellie's father leave her with Grandma?* (Because he had to work.)

- Ask: *Whose fault is it that Ellie turned into a cat?* Encourage the children to think about it then raise their hand in turn to the name 'Grandma', 'Ellie' or 'Dad'. Tell the children to organise themselves into groups of three with one person who thinks it is Grandma's fault, one person who thinks it is Ellie's fault and a third who blames Dad for creating the situation in the first place – you will probably have to ask some children to take on a different opinion for the talks.

- Ask groups to debate the question 'Whose fault is it that Ellie turned into a cat?'. Remind them to listen carefully to each other, take turns to speak, articulate their opinions and give full reasons for them.

- After a few minutes, share the children's thoughts. Hand out photocopiable page 36 'Whose fault?' and ask the children to discuss whether they agree or disagree with each statement.

- Finally, ask them to work together in their groups to come to a group decision about whose fault it is. Share their opinions as a class.

Differentiation
Extension: Ask children to share the different discussions they had with the rest of the class, explaining each other's opinions and how they changed.

4. Retell the story

Objective
To give well-structured narratives.

What you need
Copies of *Ellie and the Cat*, photocopiable page 37 'Retell the story'.

What to do

- Display an enlarged copy of photocopiable page 37 'Retell the story'. Explain that the story of *Ellie and the Cat* has become muddled and that the children are going to put it back in the correct order. Read the stages of the story together.

- Then provide pairs with individual copies of photocopiable page 37 'Retell the story' and ask them to work together to put the stages in the correct order. Ask them to cut out and stick the stages in their books, or on another piece of paper, allowing space for drawings and extra notes.

- Encourage them to find key words in the book and add these next to each stage, for example, new adjectives such as 'dingy' or 'sneaky', or two-word sentences such as 'Jolly attacks'.

- After confirming the correct sequence as a class, ask pairs to take turns to use their notes to retell the story of *Ellie and the Cat* to their partner.

- After a first attempt, share any feedback. Ask: *Could your partner hear you clearly? Did your story make sense? Was there any part of the story you missed out? What interesting words did you manage to use?* Ask them to look back at their plan and make further notes to improve their retelling.

- Share retellings as a class. (You may wish to keep children's notes to help with Assessment, page 44.)

Differentiation
Support: Invite groups to create a joint retelling, with children taking it in turns to tell the story.

Extension: Encourage children to use different techniques to hold audience attention such as changing volume, keeping eye contact and adding direct speech.

5. Hula hoop teamwork

Objective

To participate in collaborative conversations.

What you need

A hula hoop for each group.

Cross-curricular links

PE, PSHE

What to do

- Ask pairs to discuss three ways in which teamwork is important in *Ellie and the Cat*. Share ideas, for example, the spiders make a ladder, the mice make a pyramid, the cats and the mice search the garden, the mice and the spiders help Ellie search the house.

- Work in a large space. Provide groups of four or five with a hula hoop. Ask groups to hold the hula hoop between them, balancing the hoop on the top of their pointed forefingers. They then try to move the hoop from shoulder height to the floor without it losing contact with anyone's finger.

- If necessary, provide tips. (For example, one person manages the group, leaving the rest to hold the hoop; this person could count, move their finger down for everyone to follow, mark a point to go down to and so on. Children count slowly, agreeing to move the hoop down a specified amount on each count. They could count the number of times they lose contact and then try and beat this number on a second attempt.)

- After a few minutes, discuss what is tricky, for example, if one person moves their finger down too fast, then they will lose contact with the hoop; trying to keep in contact with the hoop can make the hoop rise; it's hard to kneel down while moving the hoop.

- Tell the groups to discuss solutions, carefully listening to each other's ideas.

- Afterwards, reflect on the experience. Together, discuss children's experiences of working as a team in other situations.

Differentiation

Support: Children could start in the kneeling position.

Extension: Ask groups to present their solutions to the class.

6. A hot seat for Grandma

Objectives

To participate in role play; to ask relevant questions to extend their understanding and knowledge.

What you need

Copies of *Ellie and the Cat*.

Cross-curricular link

Drama

What to do

- Remind children of their work in 'Questions for Grandma' (Plot, character and setting, page 26).

- Ask them to search *Ellie and the Cat* for facts about Grandma (Chapters 1, 2, 3, 6 and 9). Share facts: she can do magic, she has had a dragon living in her garden, she plays chess with trolls, she frowns when Ellie is rude, she thinks Jolly is a good cat, she has lost her wedding ring, and so on.

- Ask groups of four to recall their questions for Grandma from the earlier activity and add some new ones based on the facts they have found. Groups then compare questions with another group, borrowing any questions that they like.

- Ask one child in each group to take on the role of Grandma. The other group members take turns to ask the questions, with 'Grandma' attempting to answer them. Explain that 'Grandma' should use information from the text as a first source for the answers; after that, they can make up answers, but they must fit with what we know about Grandma.

- When the groups and the 'Grandmas' have asked and answered the questions, ask the children to form new groups with new children taking on the role of Grandma. Encourage them to ask 'Grandma' the questions they liked from the first role play, and new questions based on the answers given to the questions.

- Share ideas that the children have come up with about Grandma.

Differentiation

Support: Share questions and ideas about Grandma before the session.

Extension: Encourage children to give more detailed and interesting answers.

All about cats

- Use the questions and pictures below to help you plan and give a presentation about cats.

Kittens practise hunting by playing

Sphynx cat

What do kittens like to do?

What types of cat are there?

Why do cats play with their food?

What are typical cat behaviours?

How do you look after a cat?

What noises do cats make?

Grooming

Cats love to hunt

Whose fault?

- Read these statements in a group. Decide whether you agree or disagree with each statement. Remember to listen to each other.

1. Grandma should be more careful about using her magic.

2. Grandma should not have cast a spell that was so difficult to undo.

3. Grandma knew that Ellie would find the ring and learn her lesson.

4. Grandma's spell was the best thing to happen to Ellie.

5. It's not Dad's fault that he needs to work.

6. Dad should have tried harder to find a job that doesn't involve travel.

7. Dad should try harder to make Ellie feel loved and special.

8. Throwing food on the floor is a terrible thing to do.

9. Feeling sad is not a good reason to be mean to people.

10. Ellie is the one responsible for her bad temper.

11. People who are sad are often bad-tempered.

12. It is fine to be bad-tempered if you are sad.

Retell the story

- Cut out the stages of the story and arrange them in the correct order.

- Add some key words from the story.

✂

Jolly attacks the pyramid.	The mice and spiders search in the garden.
Ellie meets Dimple and Vinegar.	Ellie arrives in the car.
Grandma turns Ellie back into a girl.	Ellie helps Vinegar and Vinegar finds Grandma's ring.
Ellie throws her food on the floor.	Jolly tries to eat Dimple.
Vinegar falls into the well.	Grandma turns Ellie into a cat.

GET WRITING ▶

1. Newspaper report

Objectives
To organise paragraphs around a theme; to use simple organisational devices in a newspaper report.

What you need
Copies of *Ellie and the Cat*, age-appropriate newspaper articles.

What to do

- Share newspaper articles together and locate the key elements: a main heading; a first line that says who, what, where and when; a quotation; a photograph and a caption.

- Tell the children that they are going to create a newspaper article about the events in *Ellie and the Cat*. Discuss possible titles such as 'Wedding ring found', 'Girl turns into a cat', 'It's a catastrophe', 'A witch at large', 'A lesson learned'.

- Share ideas for a first line, for example, 'Last Saturday, Ellie Turbot (8 years old) was turned into a cat by her grandmother, 60-year-old Tilly Turbot, in the village of Redheath.' Find the 'who', the 'what', the 'when' and the 'where' in the sentence.

- Share ideas for the quotation. For example, a neighbour: 'There's always something strange going on next door – I'm sure I saw a dragon once.'; an environmental control officer: 'I was called to the scene and saw the garden overrun with cats, spiders and mice.'

- Invite the children to write their own newspaper article, adding a quotation, a picture, a caption and a paragraph of text.

Differentiation
Support: Provide children with a frame to write on.

Extension: Encourage children to give their newspaper a name and to add a second quotation from a different person.

2. A letter to Grandma

Objective
To compose and rehearse sentences orally, increasing the range of sentence structures.

What you need
A completed version of photocopiable page 22 'Choosing conjunctions'.

Cross-curricular link
PSHE

What to do

- Ask pairs to role play a conversation between Grandma and Ellie in which Ellie says sorry for her behaviour. Afterwards, discuss the vocabulary used. (For example, 'sorry', 'embarrassed', 'because', 'unloved', 'promise', 'forgive', 'friends', 'happy'.) Share some of the things that 'Ellie' and 'Grandma' said to each other.

- Use a completed version of photocopiable page 22 to recap on using the conjunctions 'because', 'if', 'when' and 'although'. Create sentences that Ellie or Grandma might say using these. (For example, 'Although you were rude, I still love you.'; 'I was rude because I was cross with Dad.'; 'I was proud when you made friends with the spiders.'; 'If you promise to be good, I promise not to turn you into a cat again.')

- Ask the children to imagine that Ellie is too shy to talk to Grandma, so she decides to write Grandma a letter. Tell the children to write this letter. Challenge them to use each of the conjunctions at least once in their letter.

Differentiation
Support: Provide children with a series of clauses such as 'because I was unhappy', 'when I threw my food on the floor', 'if I can stay here', 'although I didn't like being a cat'. Ask children to extend these into sentences and then use them in their letter.

Extension: Ask children to write a reply from Grandma.

3. Review

Objective

To write a book review after discussing the features of similar reviews.

What you need

Copies of *Ellie and the Cat*, photocopiable page 41 'Review', reviews of other books the children know.

What to do

- Organise the children into small groups, providing each group with one copy of photocopiable page 41 'Review' and copies of *Ellie and the Cat*. Ask them to discuss the book and their feelings about it, using the questions on the photocopiable sheet. Remind the children that they don't have to agree with each other, but they do have to listen to each other, making sure that everyone has a chance to speak and give their opinions. Share thoughts and opinions as a class.

- Display a review of a book that the children know well. Look at the features of the review together – the style of writing, vocabulary, structure, the introduction to the story that doesn't give away the plot, details of the story, and so on.

- Provide the children with individual copies of the photocopiable sheet. Discuss the purpose of a review. (To help someone to know if they would enjoy a particular book.) Ask: *How much of the story should we give away?* Share ideas. Agree that you might want to say that Ellie is turned into a cat and has to complete a task before she is human again.

- Ask the children to write their reviews.

- Display the reviews in the school library or book corner.

Differentiation

Support: Provide the children with sentence openers to help get them started.

Extension: Provide further examples of reviews for children to read. Expect them to mimic a suitable formal writing style.

4. A Jolly poem

Objective

To compose and rehearse sentences orally, progressively building a varied and rich vocabulary in order to write a poem.

What you need

Copies of *Ellie and the Cat*, photocopiable page 42 'A Jolly poem'.

What to do

- Display an enlarged version of photocopiable page 42 'A Jolly poem'. Read the words together and discuss the meaning of any that the children have recently learned. Discuss which things the words described in *Ellie and the Cat*. Challenge volunteers to create a sentence for key vocabulary.

- Discuss which words go well together to create half-rhymes or alliteration, such as 'dreadful and devious', 'vicious and devious', 'scampering and skidding'.

- Model using the words to create your own poem about Jolly the cat, such as: 'Jolly is dreadful and devious / Jolly is vile and vicious / Jolly is creepy and cruel / Jolly is skidding towards us / Run!' or 'Dreadful, devious, detestable / Here comes Jolly / Smirking, growling, sneering / Here comes Jolly / Spooky, dingy and dirty / Up to the attic / Scampering, skidding, shivering / Go the mice / Tumbling, trampling, terrified / Let's hide.'

- Provide individual children with the photocopiable sheet and ask them to cut out the words and to try to pair up words that go together.

- Then ask them to write their own poem about Jolly using the pairs of words and other ideas. Challenge them to create some form of pattern in their poem and to try and use some alliteration, but don't set any requirement for rhyme. Ask them to keep the words from the sheet handy for inspiration.

Differentiation

Support: Create a frame, using one of the model poems above, for the children to complete.

Extension: Challenge children to create a poem that plays with sound in most lines.

5. Jolly and the Girl

Objective
To create settings, characters and plot when writing a story.

What you need
Copies of *Ellie and the Cat*, photocopiable page 43 'Jolly and the Girl plan', photocopiable page 42 'A Jolly poem'.

What to do

- Ask a volunteer, in the character of Jolly, to take the hot seat. Together, ask 'Jolly' questions, for example: *How did you feel when Grandma shouted at you? Is it bad for cats to eat mice? Would you like to be friends with the mice? Are you happy that Ellie has come to live with Grandma?* Support 'Jolly' as she tries to answer in role.

- Hand out photocopiable page 43 'Jolly and the Girl plan' and ask the children to plan out a short story about Jolly. Agree that Jolly can still be mean, or she can be sad because no one understands her. Clarify that this can be a sequel to *Ellie and the Cat*, or the events of *Ellie and the Cat* from Jolly's point of view, or a new story. Ask: *Where will Jolly go? Who will she meet?*

- Ask the children to share completed plans with a partner and listen to their advice.

- Display an enlarged version of photocopiable page 42 'A Jolly poem' and encourage children to note down interesting words to use in each section of their story.

- Ask children to write a first version and then share with a partner. After checking for grammar and punctuation errors, and taking on any suggestions from their partner, let them create final versions to share as a class.

Differentiation
Support: Invite children to plan a story in a small group, creating a simple plot and noting down key vocabulary. Then ask the children to write the story independently using the plan.

Extension: Challenge children to add well-punctuated dialogue to their story.

6. More about cats

Objectives
To organise paragraphs around a theme; to use simple organisational devices when writing information texts.

What you need
A range of non-fiction books about cats; notes and materials from children's cat presentations (Talk about it, page 32).

What to do

- This activity extends the oral work the children did in Talk about it, page 32.

- Provide groups with non-fiction books about cats. Together, discuss the features of non-fiction texts that they find in the books and make a list on the board. (For example: heading, subheadings, captions, formal language, key words, present-tense verbs, contents, index.)

- Ask the children to recall the presentation they gave about cats. Help them to gather together any materials that they used for their presentation, copying any joint notes so that all the children in the group have access to the materials they used.

- Explain that they are going to use their notes to write a page of information covering the aspects of cats that they talked about in their presentation. Ask them to include the following features: a main heading, a one-sentence introduction, two subheadings with text and one picture with a caption.

- When complete, ask pairs to read each other's finished text and check for spelling and grammar mistakes.

- Photocopy the finished texts and gather them together in sets of different pages. Give each pair of children a set of pages and ask them to create a book with a cover and contents page.

Differentiation
Support: Create a non-fiction frame for children to use and provide them with some of the elements to populate it with (headings, text, pictures, captions).

Extension: Ask children to create a longer, more detailed page of information with three subheadings and two pictures with captions.

Review

• Did you enjoy *Ellie and the Cat*? Write a review here.

Title: ————————————————————————————————

Author: ———————————————————————————————

What is it about?

_____

_____

_____

_____

_____

_____

Who would enjoy it?

_____

_____

_____

_____

What is your favourite part?

_____

_____

_____

_____

How many stars? ☆ ☆ ☆ ☆ ☆

A Jolly poem

- Read these words that you've encountered while reading *Ellie and the Cat*.

- Cut out the words and decide which words sound good together.

✂

creep	detestable	devious	dingy
disagreeable	dreadful	dumpy	foul
frumpy	furious	gleamed	gloat
grimy	growled	grubby	horrible
impressive	jiggling	minty-flinty	padded
rumbling	scamper	shivered	skidded
slimy	slunk	smirking	snarled
sneer	spectacles	spiteful	spooky
sulked	swooped	trampled	tumbling
vicious	vile	wailed	wriggling

Jolly and the Girl plan

- Use this sheet to plan out a new story for Jolly. What will happen to her? How will she learn to be a good cat?

The story starts. What happens to Jolly?

_____

_____

_____

Where does Jolly go? Who does Jolly meet?

_____

_____

_____

What is the climax of the story? What bad thing nearly happens?

_____

_____

_____

The story ends. Where is Jolly at the end? What lesson has she learned?

_____

_____

_____

ASSESSMENT ▶

1. Vocabulary check

Objective
To build a varied and rich vocabulary.

What you need
Photocopiable page 47 'Dimple Scrunchy the seventy-fifth', dictionaries.

What to do

- Provide the children with photocopiable page 47 'Dimple Scrunchy the seventy-fifth' and ask them to read it with their partner. Clarify that this is the first time that Ellie meets Dimple, in Chapter 4.

- Write the words 'sneaky', 'boldest', 'impressive', 'devious', 'sly' on the board. Ask the children to circle these words on the sheet and check that they understand the meaning of each in context. Encourage them to use dictionaries, or a partner's knowledge, to check their understanding.

- Ask the children to: write down the three words from the list that have a similar meaning to each other ('sneaky', 'devious', 'sly'); write a definition for the word 'sly' (for example, behaving in a secretive way; planning to do harm to others); list three things that can be described as 'impressive' (for example, a large building, a high score on a game); complete the sentence 'Jolly is devious because…'; describe a time that Jolly behaves in a 'sneaky' way; answer the question 'How does Dimple behave in the 'boldest' way?'

- Use the children's answers to assess their understanding of the new vocabulary learned and their ability to use it themselves.

Differentiation

Support: Create definition cards for 'impressive' (amazing), 'boldest' (most brave) and 'devious' (secretively behaving in a bad way). Children match the words and the definition.

Extension: Children write their own sentences including 'impressive', 'boldest' and 'devious'.

2. In the morning

Objective
To use fronted adverbials.

What you need
Copies of *Ellie and the Cat*, children's notes from Talk about it, page 33 (optional).

What to do

- Remind the children of previous work on fronted adverbials and ask them to suggest a range of fronted adverbials. Write ideas on the board then circle those to do with time (For example: 'All of a sudden,'; 'As the sun was setting,'; 'At last,'). Write these on the board with their associated comma.

- Ask the children to write a series of sentences, each of which starts with a fronted adverbial, to tell the story of *Ellie and the Cat*. Provide copies of *Ellie and the Cat* for inspiration, explaining that they can use phrases from the story, or use their own phrases. Agree that they should have at least one sentence for each chapter. For example: 'When Ellie arrived at Grandma's, she was in a bad mood. At dinner, Ellie threw her food on the floor. Finally, Grandma lost her temper and put a spell on Ellie. At once, Ellie became small and furry.'

- Assess the children's ability to use fronted adverbials for time, to use a comma after a fronted adverbial and to understand the key elements of the plot.

Differentiation

Support: Provide the children with their notes from their oral retelling of the story (Talk about it, page 33) to help them remember the plot. Display a list of fronted adverbials to choose from.

Extension: Ask the children to create a series of sentences that flow together to tell the story.

3. Because she was cross

Objectives
To extend the range of sentences with more than one clause by using a wider range of conjunctions including 'when', 'if', 'because', 'although'; to understand what they read in books they can read independently.

What to do

- Ask the children to answer the following questions. Tell them that they must use the given conjunction in their answer:

  - *Why does Grandma turn Ellie into a cat?* (because) (For example, 'Grandma turns Ellie into a cat because she wants Ellie to learn some manners.')
  - *When does Ellie start to feel embarrassed about her behaviour?* (when) (Ellie starts to feel embarrassed about her behaviour when she talks to Dimple and Vinegar.)
  - *Why is Ellie so rude at the beginning of the story?* (because) (Ellie is rude to Grandma because she is cross and upset about being abandoned by her father.)
  - *Why is it hard for Ellie to decide to rescue Vinegar?* (if) (If Ellie rescues Vinegar, she will have to stop looking for the ring.)
  - *When does Vinegar find the ring?* (when) (Vinegar finds the ring when she falls in the well.)
  - *How will Ellie become a girl again?* (if) (Ellie will become a girl again if she finds Grandma's ring before Grandma finishes dinner.)
  - *How does Grandma feel about Ellie?* (although) (Although Grandma does not like Ellie's behaviour, she loves Ellie.)
  - *When does Jolly lie to Grandma?* (when) (Jolly lies to Grandma when she tells Grandma that she wants to help Ellie find the ring.)

- Assess both children's understanding of the story and their ability to correctly use 'because', 'if', 'when' and 'although'.

Differentiation
Support: Reduce the number of questions that you require children to answer. Focus on one question for each conjunction.

Extension: Challenge children to write new questions for their classmates.

4. Meet Dimple

Objective
To prepare a section of the novel to read aloud and to perform, showing understanding through intonation, tone, volume and action.

What you need
Photocopiable page 47 'Dimple Scrunchy the seventy-fifth'.

Cross-curricular link
Drama

What to do

- Hand out photocopiable page 47 'Dimple Scrunchy the seventy-fifth'. Explain that the children are going to work in groups of three to prepare a dramatic reading of the text (one as the narrator, one as Ellie and one as Dimple).

- Ask children to do the following to help them prepare an interesting performance:

  - Highlight characters' speech in different colours.
  - Check the meaning of words and phrases, such as 'at your service', 'knock my block off'.
  - Practise the pronunciation of tricky words and phrases such as 'Scrunchy the seventy-fifth'.
  - Discuss the character of Dimple. (How does he talk? How might he behave? What does he think about himself? What does he think about Ellie? How might the children show these feelings with their voices? What arm movements might Dimple use as he is talking – particularly as he is introducing himself?)
  - How does Ellie feel at different points in the text? How will the children show this in their voices?
  - Discuss if any lines should be said quietly or more loudly.

- Ask groups to practise their performance. Let them swap roles before choosing a final version.

- As you listen to the children's performances, assess their understanding of the character of Dimple and the vocabulary used, along with their ability to use their voice to create drama and meaning.

Differentiation
Extension: Challenge children to perform another scene from the book.

5. Dimple Scrunchy

Objective
To identify themes and conventions.

What you need
Copies of *Ellie and the Cat*, photocopiable page 47 'Dimple Scrunchy the seventy-fifth'.

Cross-curricular link
PSHE

What to do

- Display Photocopiable page 47 'Dimple Scrunchy the seventy-fifth'. Ask: *Why is this an important scene?* (Ellie meets Dimple.) Read the text aloud, using all your skills to emphasise the character of the bold, polite Dimple. Perhaps take a bow when he introduces himself.

- Ask the children to draw a picture of Dimple in the middle of a piece of paper. Ask: *How will he look: proud and brave or shy and scared?*

- Ask the children to draw four boxes around Dimple and to label them 'Friends', 'Being brave', 'Teamwork' and 'Manners'. Agree that these are four themes that are important in the story.

- Ask the children to write a sentence in each box explaining how Dimple is important to each theme.

- Afterwards, ask volunteers to share their sentences. (For example, Friends: Dimple is Ellie's first friend; Dimple helps Ellie even when he doesn't want Jolly back; Dimple doesn't stop helping Ellie until the ring is found. Being brave: Dimple is very brave; he stands up to Ellie when he thinks she is Jolly, singing a song and making a big shadow; he doesn't run away when Jolly attacks him and his friends at the end. Teamwork: he calls on the other mice to help; he helps search the garden and make a mouse pyramid. Manners: Dimple has lovely manners; he helps Ellie to see her own rudeness as silly.)

- As the children present their findings, assess their ability to identify the themes running through the book.

Differentiation

Support: Ask children to focus on how Dimple is an important friend to Ellie.

Extension: Ask children to write two sentences for each theme.

6. Jolly the sorry

Objectives
To predict what might happen from details stated and implied; to use and punctuate direct speech.

What you need
Copies of *Ellie and the Cat*.

What to do

- Ask the children to turn to a partner and discuss whether they think Jolly will have decided to change for ever at the end of the story, or just be more careful when attacking the mice. Listen to the children as they talk and assess which children are able to engage with the character of Jolly (who will just be more devious) or the theme of the book (Jolly will be made to behave better). Can the children use 'because' to explain their thoughts?

- Tell the children to discuss ideas for a new scene in which Jolly meets Dimple Scrunchy a few hours after the events of the story have finished. Ask: *What will they say to each other? Will Jolly ask to be friends? Will she try and catch Dimple? Will Dimple introduce her to the mice? Will Dimple try and wake Ellie?* Point out that the partners do not need to choose the same scenario but do need to help each other clarify their ideas by listening and making suggestions.

- Ask the children to write a short scene, remembering to use correct punctuation for direct speech. Children can refer to the text to find words for how the animals move and ideas for how they talk.

- Afterwards, ask volunteers to read their scene out loud.

- Assess the children's ability to correctly punctuate speech and to engage with the characters from the story.

Differentiation

Support: Support children as they develop their scenario. Recap on the rules of direct speech before they write independently.

Extension: Ask children to extend their writing into a longer scene and introduce new characters.

Dimple Scrunchy the seventy-fifth

"Arrgh!" said a voice. "Jolly the giant! I've had it now."

Ellie looked down to where the voice was coming from. "Who are you?" she asked, surprised.

"Dimple Scrunchy the seventy-fifth – at your service!" said the mouse in front of Ellie.

"But you're a mouse!" Ellie said.

"Of course I'm a mouse," said Dimple. "Go on, Jolly the sneaky, get it over with. Don't play with me! Just knock my block off!" Dimple closed his eyes and stuck out his neck.

Ellie frowned. "Why on earth would I do that?" she asked.

Dimple opened his eyes and stared at her without saying a word.

"Was it you who made that giant shadow?" Ellie asked as she raised a paw to point at the wall.

"I did," Dimple said slowly. "I make the biggest, boldest shadow, don't you think?"

"Yes, I do," Ellie said. "It's very impressive, especially for a mouse. I thought you were at least as big as an elephant."

Dimple looked Ellie over. "Who are you?" he asked. "You look like Jolly the devious, but you don't sound like her. And you're not very smart, are you? Mind you, I've never met a cat who was smart. Sly, yes. Smart, no."

"I'm not a cat," Ellie said. "I'm a girl!"

"Does that mean you're not going to eat me?" Dimple asked hopefully.

"Ugh! Eat you? I don't think so!" Ellie shivered at the thought of eating a mouse.

Dimple breathed a sigh of relief. "Now I know you're not Jolly the sly," Dimple said. "She would have swallowed me in two seconds flat. So how did you come to look like Jolly the nasty?"

"Grandma put me in Jolly's body because I …" Ellie began. "I threw my food on the floor." She felt very silly saying it.

SCHOLASTIC

READ & RESPOND

Available in this series:

978-1407-15879-2

978-1407-14224-1

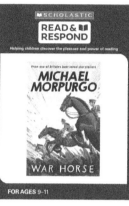

978-1407-16063-4

978-1407-16056-6

978-1407-14228-9

978-1407-16069-6

978-1407-16070-2

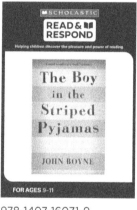

978-1407-16071-9

978-1407-14230-2

978-1407-16057-3

978-1407-16064-1

978-1407-14223-4

978-0702-30890-1

978-0702-30859-8

To find out more,
visit www.scholastic.co.uk/read-and-respond